Dumb.

COOL
PAPER ART

ORIGAMI

CLASSIC
PAPER FOLDING

RACHAEL L.
THOMAS

Checkerboard
Library

An Imprint of Abdo Publishing
abdobooks.com

abdobooks.com

Published by Abdo Publishing, a division of ABDO, PO Box 398166, Minneapolis, Minnesota 55439. Copyright © 2020 by Abdo Consulting Group, Inc. International copyrights reserved in all countries. No part of this book may be reproduced in any form without written permission from the publisher. Checkerboard Library™ is a trademark and logo of Abdo Publishing.

Printed in the United States of America, North Mankato, Minnesota
052019
092019

THIS BOOK CONTAINS
RECYCLED MATERIALS

Design: Christa Schneider, Mighty Media, Inc.
Production: Mighty Media, Inc.
Editor: Liz Salzmann
Cover Photographs: Mighty Media, Inc.
Interior Photographs: iStockphoto, pp. 5, 29; Mighty Media, Inc., pp. 1, 3, 4 (pattern), 7 (all), 8–27 (all), 28 (pattern, googly eyes), 30, 31, 32; Shutterstock Images, pp. 4–5, 6 (all), 28 (rabbit, boat)

The following manufacturers/names appearing in this book are trademarks: Crayola®, Scotch®

Library of Congress Control Number: 2018966250

Publisher's Cataloging-in-Publication Data
Names: Thomas, Rachael L., author.
Title: Origami: classic paper folding / by Rachael L. Thomas.
Description: Minneapolis, Minnesota : Abdo Publishing, 2020 | Series: Cool paper art | Includes online resources and index.
Identifiers: ISBN 9781532119460 (lib. bdg.) | ISBN 9781532173929 (ebook)
Subjects: LCSH: Paper art--Juvenile literature. | Origami--Juvenile literature. | Japanese paper folding--Juvenile literature. | Paper folding (Handicraft)--Juvenile literature.
Classification: DDC 736.982--dc23

CONTENTS

Ancient Paper Folding   4
Origami Paper   6
Origami Basics   8
Curious Cat   10
Cool Ice Cream Cone   **12**
Sharp Shirt and Tie   14
Dazzling Dress   **18**
Tremendous Tree   22
Climbing Koala   **24**
Conclusion   28
Glossary   30
Online Resources   31
Index   32

ANCIENT PAPER FOLDING

Origami is an ancient form of art using paper. The word comes from the Japanese words *oru*, meaning "fold," and *kami*, meaning "paper." Origami artists make models of animals, plants, people and many more amazing things.

Origami wouldn't exist without paper. Paper was invented 2,000 years ago in China. Around 500 CE, **Buddhist** monks brought paper from China to Japan. Japan is where the art of paper folding became what we know today as origami.

At first, only the richest people in Japan could practice origami. This was because paper was very expensive at the time. So, most people couldn't afford it.

Then, as the paper industry improved, paper became less expensive. More and more Japanese people were able to make origami. People began to make origami models as decorations and sent them to others as gifts. Origami was also used to teach math.

Origami remains an important part of Japanese **culture**. But now origami is also practiced all around the world in many different ways. Anyone can become an origami master, including you!

ORIGAMI PAPER

Most origami is made from one square piece of origami paper. This paper is often thinner than regular paper. The paper's thinness makes it easier to fold multiple times.

But it is possible to make origami with any paper you have on hand. Origami artists are known to work with all kinds of materials. You can make origami using leftover wrapping paper or scrapbook paper. Some people use paper that would otherwise be thrown away or recycled. This includes newspapers, magazines, and junk mail.

Origami squares are usually 6 by 6 inches (15 by 15 cm). If you are cutting your own origami squares, you can use these **dimensions**. Or you can make squares that are larger or smaller. Just make sure that all four sides are the same length.

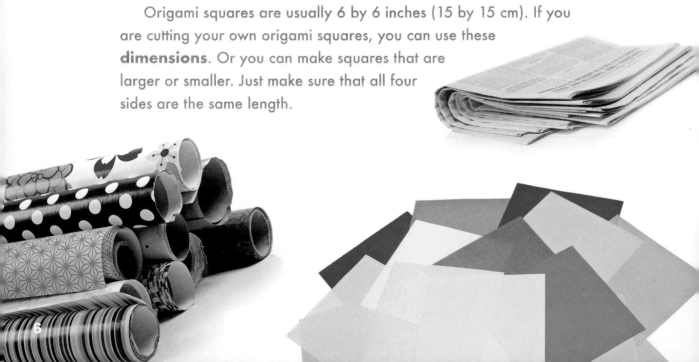

ADDITIONAL SUPPLIES

bone folder

craft stick

tape

glue

scissors

marker

TIPS & TRICKS

Follow the instructions very carefully. It is important to do the steps in the correct order! Also, remember to be patient. Work slowly and don't worry if you make a mistake. Just unfold the paper and try again. It takes a lot of practice to become an origami expert.

ORIGAMI BASICS

Mastering basic **techniques** will help you move quickly and easily through the steps of building origami models. Here are a few of the most common origami folds.

Valley Fold
Fold the paper in front like a valley.

Mountain Fold
Fold the paper behind like a mountain.

Crease
Press firmly along a fold.

Inside Reverse Fold

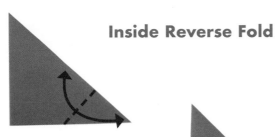

1

Fold a square piece of paper into a triangle. Valley fold one of the points. Unfold.

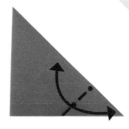

2

Mountain fold the crease. Unfold.

3

Unfold the paper. Place it so the center crease is vertical. Valley fold the bottom point on the corner crease.

4

Refold the center crease.

COMMON ORIGAMI SYMBOLS

– – – – – – – –	Valley fold
–·–·–·–·–·–·–	Mountain fold
——————	Crease
——————	Cut line
↤–––––↦	Fold and unfold
↪↬↬↬↬↬↪	Turn over
↻	Rotate
⟶	Pull or push

9

CURIOUS CAT

- square paper
- marker

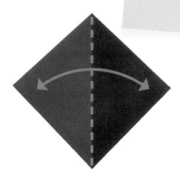

1

Place the paper on the table with a point on the top. Your cat will be the color of the facedown side. Valley fold the left point to the right point. Unfold.

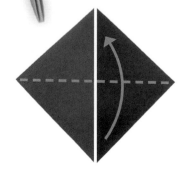

2

Valley fold the bottom point to the top point.

3

Valley fold the bottom edges to the center crease.

10

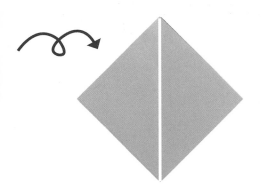

4

Turn the paper over
from side to side.

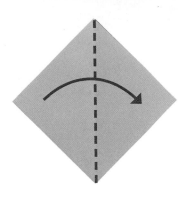

5

Valley fold the left point
to the right point.

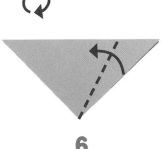

6

Rotate the paper to
the right. Valley fold
the right edge to the
center.

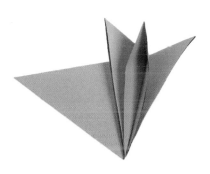

7

Lift the edge you folded
in step 6. You should see
three separate layers.

8

Fold the point of the
middle layer down into
a diamond shape.

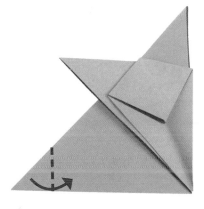

9

Fold the left point over
to make a tail.

10

Use a marker to draw
the cat's face.

COOL ICE CREAM CONE

- **square paper**

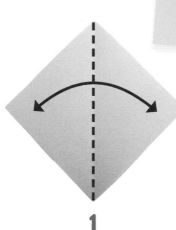

1

Place the paper on the table with a point on the top. Your ice cream cone will be the color of the facedown side. Valley fold the left point to the right point. Unfold.

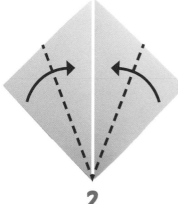

2

Valley fold the bottom edges to the center crease.

3

Valley fold the inner points outward. This makes triangles that hang over the edges of the cone.

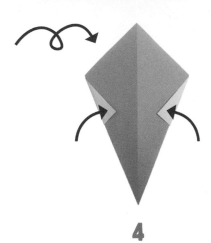

4

Turn the paper over from side to side. Valley fold the overhanging triangles over the edges of the cone.

5

Valley fold the top edges to the center crease.

6

Valley fold the top point down.

8

Valley fold the point back down. The tip should be slightly below the previous fold.

7

Valley fold the point back up. The fold should be slightly below the top edge.

9

Valley fold the point back up so it sticks up past the top edge.

10

Turn the paper over to see your finished origami ice cream cone.

SHARP SHIRT AND TIE

- 2 pieces of paper
- scissors
- ruler

SHIRT

1

Cut a rectangle and a square out of paper. The rectangle should be 6 by 8 inches (15 x 20 cm). The square should be 2½ inches (6 cm) on each side.

2

Place the rectangle on the table with a short edge at the top. Your shirt will be the color of the facedown side. Valley fold the rectangle from left to right. Unfold.

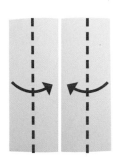

3
Valley fold the left and right edges in to the center crease.

4
Valley fold the top inner corners outward. The points should stick out past the edges of the rectangle.

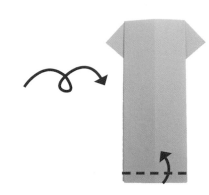

5
Turn the paper over from side to side. Valley fold the bottom edge about ½ inch (1.3 cm).

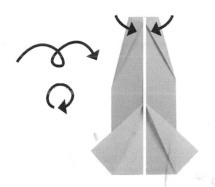

6
Turn the paper over from side to side. Rotate it so the square end is at the top. Valley fold the top corners to the center crease.

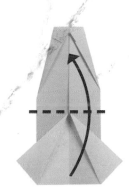

7
Valley fold the bottom up.

8
Tuck the edge under the top corners. Your origami shirt is finished.

Continued on the next page.

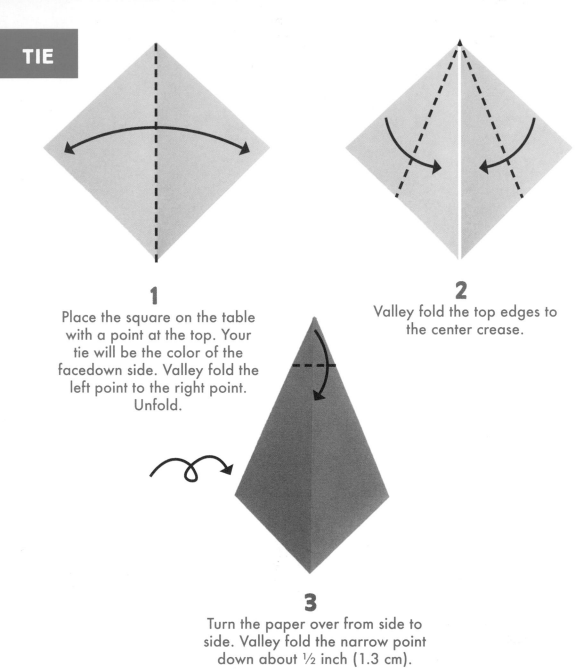

1

Place the square on the table with a point at the top. Your tie will be the color of the facedown side. Valley fold the left point to the right point. Unfold.

2

Valley fold the top edges to the center crease.

3

Turn the paper over from side to side. Valley fold the narrow point down about ½ inch (1.3 cm).

4

Valley fold the point up to the top edge of the paper.

5

Valley fold the bottom of the flap. The edge of the flap should be slightly above the top.

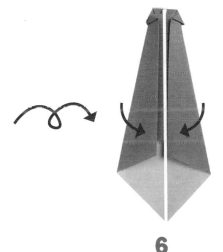

6

Turn the paper over from side to side. Valley fold the left and right edges to the center crease.

7

Your origami tie is finished. Pull the small triangle out from behind the fold. Hook it over the top of the shirt under the collar.

DAZZLING DRESS

- square paper
- ruler

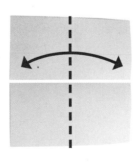

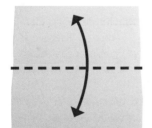

1

Place the paper on the table with a straight edge at the top. Your dress will be the color of the facedown side. Valley fold the top edge to the bottom edge. Unfold.

2

Valley fold the left edge to the right edge. Unfold.

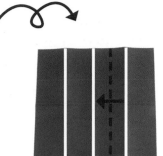

3
Valley fold the left and right edges to the center crease. Unfold.

4
Turn the paper over from side to side. Pinch the first crease in from the right. Valley fold it to the center crease.

5
Pinch the first crease in´ from the left. Valley fold it to the center crease.

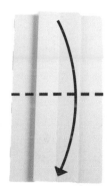

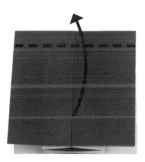

6
Turn the paper over from side to side. Valley fold the top edge to the bottom edge.

7
Valley fold the top layer back up. The fold should be about ½ inch (1.3 cm) from the top edge.

Continued on the next page.

8

Turn the paper over from side to side. Pull the two bottom rectangles outward. The bottom edge should be stretched out completely. This is the skirt of the dress.

9

Turn the paper over from side to side. Valley fold the inner left and right corners to the center crease. Unfold.

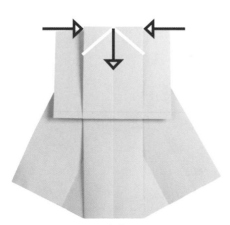

10

Lift the top layer and push the corners together. Press them flat in a diamond shape.

11

Valley fold the middle corners
into small triangles.

12

Valley fold the left edge to the
center crease. Fold the top first,
then the skirt. The crease of the
skirt should lead to the bottom
left corner of the paper.

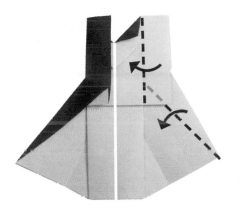

13

Repeat step 12 with
the right edge.

14

Valley fold the top inner
corners outward. The points
should stick out past the edges
of the rectangle.

15

Turn the paper over
to see your finished
origami dress.

TREMENDOUS TREE

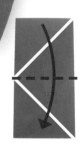

- square paper
- scissors
- glitter pom-pom
- glue

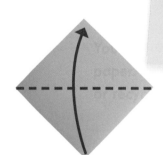

1
Place the paper on the table with a point at the top. Your tree will be the color of the facedown side. Valley fold the bottom point to the top point.

2
Valley fold the left point to the right point. Crease firmly.

3
Unfold the paper. Place it on the table with a straight edge at the top. Valley fold the left edge to the right edge.

4
Valley fold the top edge to the bottom edge. Crease firmly. Unfold the paper. Place it on the table with a point at the top.

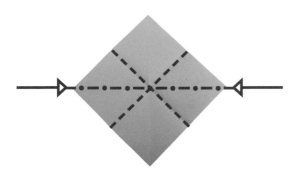

5

Pinch the folds at the left and right points. Bring them toward each other until they meet over the bottom point. Fold the top point down over them. This will form a square. Crease firmly.

6

Place the square on the table so that it opens at the bottom.

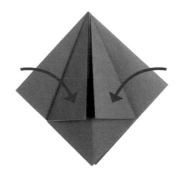

7

Valley fold the left and right edges of the top layer to the center crease. This makes two triangles.

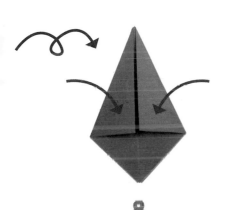

8

Turn the paper over from side to side. Valley fold the left and right edges to the center crease. This makes two more triangles.

9

Open each of the four triangles and fold them inside out.

10

Press the folds flat. Cut from the left point to the center crease at an angle. Cut from the right point to the center crease at an angle. Spread the folds apart to stand up your origami tree.

CLIMBING KOALA

- 2 pieces of paper
- scissors
- ruler
- glue
- marker

HEAD

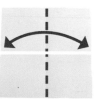

1

Cut two squares of paper the same color. Make one 3 inches (7.5 cm) square. Make the other 6 inches (15 cm) square.

2

Place the small square on the table with a straight edge at the top. Your koala's head will be the color of the facedown side. Valley fold the top edge to the bottom edge. Unfold.

3

Valley fold the left edge to the right edge. Unfold.

24

4

Valley fold the right corners to the center crease.

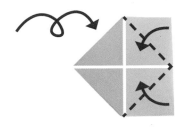

5

Turn the paper over from side to side. Valley fold the right corners to the center crease.

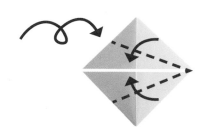

6

Turn the paper over from top to bottom. Valley fold the right edges to the center crease.

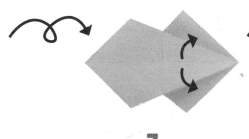

7

Turn the paper over from top to bottom. Unfold the flaps.

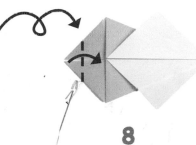

8

Turn the paper over from top to bottom. Valley fold the left point to the center crease.

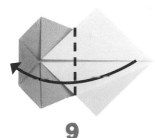

9

Valley fold the right point to the left edge. Turn the paper over. Your koala's head is finished.

BODY

1

Place the large square on the table with a point at the top. Your koala's body will be the color of the facedown side.

2

Valley fold the left point to the right point. Unfold. Valley fold the top point to the bottom point. Unfold.

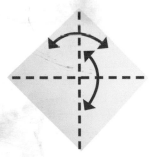

Continued on the next page.

25

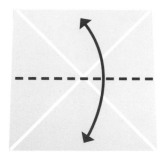

3

Rotate the square so a straight edge is at the top. Valley fold the top edge to the bottom edge. Unfold.

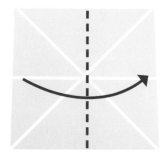

4

Valley fold the left edge to the right edge.

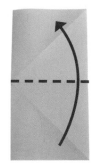

5

Valley fold the bottom edge to the top edge.

6

Place your finger on the right side of the square under the top layer. Lift the top left corner and push it toward the bottom right corner. The layer should naturally fold down into a triangle shape.

7

Turn the paper over from top to bottom. Lift the top layer of the bottom right corner and push it toward the top right corner. This completes the triangle.

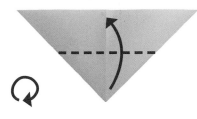

8

Rotate the triangle so the long edge is at the top. Valley fold the bottom point to the top edge.

9

Lift the top layer of the long edge. Press it open while pushing the two inner points outward. Flatten the folds.

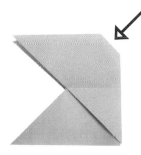

10

Valley fold the right side over the left side.

11

Make an inside reverse fold in the top right corner (see page 9).

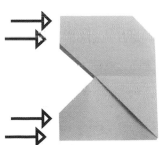

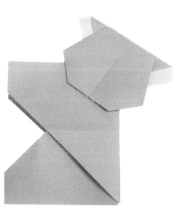

12

Make inside reverse folds in all four points to make feet.

13

Glue the head to the body. Use a marker to draw the koala's face.

CONCLUSION

The art of origami has grown from a ceremonial practice in ancient Japan to something that anyone can try! Becoming an origami artist takes practice. Repeat simple folds and models until you know them by heart. Then move on to more **complicated** folds and models.

As you master the basics, don't forget to have fun with this traditional craft. Add googly eyes, chenille stems and other decorations to bring your origami to life. You could also throw an origami party to share your origami knowledge.

And like a true artist, keep your eyes and ears open for new sources of inspiration. There are thousands of online videos showing master origami makers at work. Experiment with different materials and designs. One day, you could be the one showing your paper art to the world!

GLOSSARY

bone folder – a handheld tool used to fold and crease paper.

Buddhist – one who believes in the teachings of Gautama Buddha.

complicated – having elaborately combined parts.

culture – the customs, arts, and tools of a nation or a people at a certain time.

dimension – the measurement of extension in one direction. Length, width, and height are all dimensions.

technique (tehk-NEEK) – a method or style in which something is done.

ONLINE RESOURCES

Booklinks
NONFICTION NETWORK
FREE! ONLINE NONFICTION RESOURCES

To learn more about origami, please visit
abdobooklinks.com or scan this QR code. These links
are routinely monitored and updated to provide the most
current information available.

INDEX

B
Buddhism, 4

C
cat project, 10, 11
China, 4
common origami symbols, 9

D
dress project, 18, 19, 20, 21

I
ice cream cone project, 12, 13

J
Japan, 4, 5, 28

K
koala project, 24, 25, 26, 27

M
materials, 6, 7, 28

O
origami folds, 8, 9
origami paper, 6

P
paper, history of, 4, 5, 28

S
shirt and tie project, 14, 15, 16, 17

T
tree project, 22, 23